THE MILLENNIUM

TRANSPORTATION

A Pictorial History of the Past One Thousand Years

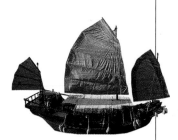

John Hamilton

ABDO
& Daughters

Visit us at
www.abdopub.com

Published by ABDO Publishing Company, 4940 Viking Drive, Edina, MN 55435.
Copyright ©2000 by Abdo Consulting Group, Inc. International copyrights
reserved in all countries. No part of this book may be reproduced in any form
without written permission from the publisher.

Printed in the United States.

Contributing Editors: Bob Italia, Tamara Britton, Kate Furlong
Art Direction: Pat Laurel, John Hamilton

Cover photos: AP/Wideworld Photos, Corbis
Interior photos: AP/Wideworld Photos, Corbis

Library of Congress Cataloging-in-Publication Data

Hamilton, John, 1959-
    Transportation/John Hamilton.
        p. cm. -- (The Millennium)
    Includes index.
    Summary: A pictorial history of developments in transportation over the last millennium.
    ISBN: 1-57765-361-0
    1. Transportation--Juvenile literature. [1. Transportation--History.] I. Title.

HE152 .H26 2000
388 21--dc21

99-043241

CONTENTS

Invented in the late 1800s, the automobile remains the most popular form of transportation in modern civilizations.

INTRODUCTION

Most animals can move from one place to another. Some, including humans, can transport goods with them during their travels. But human transportation differs from all other forms in one important way. Humans can use technology to take advantage of natural forces.

Humans have used transportation to build great civilizations. When farmers and manufacturers can easily get their goods to market, when citizens and soldiers can easily move from city to city, civilizations thrive. At the end of the millennium, humans continued to search for new ways to travel faster and carry more goods than ever before.

The age of railroads began in the early 1800s, when steam-driven trains first ran on tracks.

In some countries, bicycles are the chief means of getting around in crowded cities.

Travel by Land

Before the invention of trains and automobiles, animal power was the main form of travel in the millennium. Horses, donkeys, and oxen pulled wagons, coaches, and buggies.

Travel by Sea

Ships were used for transportation long before the millennium. By the early sixteenth century, sailing vessels began regularly traveling across the oceans, exploring the world, and transporting goods from rich, new markets. At the end of the millennium, supertankers and cruise ships could move more goods and people than ever before.

For most of the millennium, people used ships powered by sails.

The largest cruise ships can carry more than 3,000 passengers.

Travel by Air

Air travel is a recent development of the past millennium. It began with the hot air balloon in 1783. But the greatest advance was the airplane, an invention of the twentieth century. At the end of the millennium, many people in the Western world traveled by air when they needed to cover a great distance in a short amount of time.

Space shuttles ferry people and equipment into orbit around Earth.

The biggest airplanes can carry more than 400 passengers from Europe to North America without stopping.

BEFORE THE MILLENNIUM

A travois is two poles tied together to form an upside-down V, with the point resting on the back of a person or animal.

At the beginning of human history, people were nomads. They hunted animals and gathered food in order to survive. When the resources in one area ran out, they moved. Early peoples invented new ways to carry their possessions from place to place. Sticks with bundles on one end could be carried over the shoulder. Y-shaped sledges, called *travois*, were used to pull heavy loads, either by human or animal power.

Eventually, people had to find a way to move across water. Sailing ships appeared in ancient Egypt around 4000 B.C. As shipbuilding technology improved, bigger and better hulls were constructed and oars were added.

An ancient stone wheel discovered in Turkey

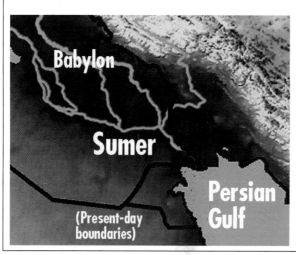

Prehistoric peoples invented the wheel. The first wheeled vehicle, a two-wheeled cart, appeared in Sumer (present-day Iraq) around 3500 B.C.

Early wheeled vehicles gave rise to animal-powered chariots and wagons, allowing people to travel far from their homes. This helped them build great empires.

Animals were first ridden around the second millennium B.C. But it was the invention of saddlery that made animals a practical means of transportation.

Chariots

Chariots were most commonly fast, lightweight, two-wheeled vehicles used in war, racing, parades, travel, and hunting. They first appeared in Sumer around 3000 B.C. The Chinese, Syrian, Assyrian, Egyptian, Greek, and Roman militaries used them to establish their empires.

Sumerian chariots (left) had four wooden wheels. The chariots were pulled by oxen and were heavy and slow.

Chariots were designed to hold a driver and a warrior. The first chariots had a framework of wood covered with skins. Later versions were made of wood and bronze.

In the second millennium B.C., Assyrians added two horses and bronze-spoked wheels to their chariots to increase speed (left). The added swiftness and mobility helped them dominate the Middle East until 600 B.C.

Though the cavalry eventually replaced the war chariot, the Greeks and Romans still used chariots for racing and parades.

Horse Equipment

In the second millennium B.C., the nomadic people of Asia were the first to ride horses bareback. Riding bareback made it difficult for riders to keep their balance and it also gave them little control over the horse. The bridle was invented in Syria in the fourteenth century B.C. This allowed the rider to control the horse's movements and behavior. The saddle, invented by the Scythians in the fifth century B.C., improved the rider's balance. The first saddles were two hides sewn together and padded with horse hair. By the fifth century A.D., stirrups had been invented, which gave riders more stability and allowed them to travel faster and further without tiring quickly.

This ochre on stone painting, found in Algeria, shows men riding horses that have crude saddles.

Caravans

Caravans were important in ancient Asia and Africa. They helped distribute scarce goods like silk and spices. People traveling in caravans exchanged knowledge and ideas between empires. Many wars were fought to control the best caravan routes.

A camel caravan crosses a desert in southern China.

In mountainous parts of the world, llamas and donkeys were often used in caravans. Camels were used in dry countries, since they could carry heavy loads and go without water for long distances. Large caravans could stretch as long as six miles (10 km).

In lands that are frozen much of the time, dogs are used to pull sleds.

Elephants have long been used as transportation in Africa and Asia. Though elephants need to drink up to 40 gallons (151 liters) of water each day, they can carry heavy loads over rough terrain.

As animal-drawn carts and wagons became more common, the need for roads increased. Some of the earliest civilizations to build networks of roads included the Chinese, the Inca, and the Romans. The first and most famous of Roman roads is the Via Appia (left), which was built in 312 B.C.

Early Ships

By 4000 B.C., Egyptians were building ships with wooden hulls and simple rectangular sails. As trade between countries became more important, shipbuilding technology steadily improved. Rowing vessels, such as Greek triremes of the fifth century B.C., gave way to more advanced sailing ships. Major improvements included better types of sails, sternpost rudders, and magnetic compasses, allowing ships to cover vast distances away from the sight of land.

To transport themselves over water, prehistoric peoples used floating logs, rafts, and inflated animal skins.

Native Americans and the Inuit developed the canoe. Native Americans made canoes from birch bark (left). The Inuit stretched animal skins over wooden frames.

The largest of the Viking longships (below) of about A.D. 800 had 64 oars and were up to 78 feet long (24 m). The Vikings used these ships to raid coastal villages and explore the far reaches of the North Atlantic.

The Chinese invented a seaworthy boat called a junk (above). By the ninth century A.D., junks were carrying Chinese explorers all the way to India and Indonesia.

ANIMAL TRANSPORT

At the beginning of the millennium, people rode animals and used them to pull wagons. But riding bareback was difficult, and wagons were not comfortable to ride in. Advances in saddlery made riding animals easier. Then came the introduction of coaches and buggies that had more comfortable suspension. People used animals for their transportation needs for many years. By the end of the millennium, other methods of transportation had replaced animals in modern civilizations. Animals remained popular for recreational riding.

From the turn of the millennium to about the seventeenth century, most Europeans used large, powerful horses for military mounts and for hauling heavy loads.

At the end of the 1600s, fast Arabian stallions (below) were brought to England and France, where they were bred with native stock.

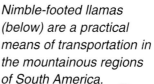

Camels (below), which can store water in their bodies for long periods of time, are used for travel in the world's desert regions.

Nimble-footed llamas (below) are a practical means of transportation in the mountainous regions of South America.

Saddles

In the Middle Ages, with armored knights riding into combat as "shock troops" (right), leather saddles became larger and heavier so they could be used as platforms from which to attack ground soldiers. This allowed riders to wield their swords with more control. In the late 1800s and early 1900s, as horses became less important in warfare, saddles became lighter.

Horses were brought to the Americas by Spanish conquistadores Hernán Cortés and Hernando de Soto during their explorations. These are the ancestors of herds found in western North America (right) and used by Native Americans.

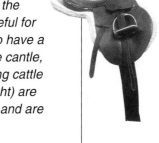

Modern saddles come in two main types. The Western saddle (left) has a high horn on the pommel, in front of the rider, which is useful for tying down lariats. Western saddles also have a raised area in back of the rider called the cantle, which gives firm seat support when roping cattle and other livestock. English saddles (right) are lighter and flatter than Western saddles, and are used mostly for sport riding.

Mules (left) are used to transport people to the floor of the Grand Canyon in Arizona. Elephants (below) are used as urban transportation in Asia and Africa.

Wagons and Coaches

At the beginning of the millennium, animal-drawn wagons were used primarily to haul cargo. Covered wagons were used in Asia, the Middle East, and Europe during the Middle Ages to transport goods and people, but the ride was bumpy and uncomfortable.

Coaches first appeared in Hungary in the 1400s. Their use by royalty and the wealthy slowly spread throughout Europe. Road improvements in the 1600s allowed coach service between towns. Coach bodies were carved for a more appealing look. Glass windows were added in the late 1600s.

Horse-drawn coach wagons were more comfortable for passengers because the body was suspended on the chassis by straps, which made the ride much less jarring.

Invented about 1660, Berlin coaches (right) had two-perch running gear and thoroughbrace suspension.

Conestoga wagons (below) were invented in Pennsylvania in the early 1700s to carry furs from fur-trading posts to market. In the 1800s, they helped transport American settlers and their belongings west across the frontier. With a bed length of up to 16 feet (5 m), these wagons were pulled by teams of up to six horses or 10 oxen. Nicknamed "prairie schooners," these long and sleek covered wagons were often seen crossing America's Great Plains.

The coach's suspension improved in the 1700s, with the addition of springs. Toward the late 1700s, coaches appeared in North American cities. Stagecoaches became an increasingly important form of transportation as roads steadily improved. By the early 1800s, stagecoach service provided the only means of cross-country travel for Americans. The age of the coach did not end until the appearance of the mass-produced automobile in the early 1900s.

Stagecoach routes were divided into "stages" where passengers could get on or off. Horse teams had to be replaced about every 10 miles (16 km). Stagecoaches also transported mail.

Buggies (right) first appeared in the late 1800s. Smaller, lighter, and less expensive than coaches, buggies were the most widely-used vehicles in America until the appearance of the automobile.

In many parts of the world, horses are still used for pulling heavy loads or carriages.

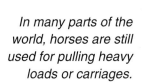

SHIPS

During the age of exploration, the oceans were perceived as dangerous and filled with monsters.

At the beginning of the past millennium, several technologies came together to open up the oceans to exploration. The magnetic compass first appeared on Western vessels around the year 1000. This reduced the chance of getting lost at sea and encouraged development of bigger, ocean-going ships. Triangular lateen sails, which could take wind on either side, became popular. Sternpost rudders were introduced around 1200, making ships much easier to steer.

The age of the sail lasted until the 1800s, when steamboats first appeared. Iron and steel hulls replaced wooden ones and led to the development of the mighty vessels used at the end of the millennium.

The magnetic compass

The carrack, like this replica of one of Christopher Columbus's ships (right), was outfitted with three or four masts, some of which had platforms where soldiers could shoot down on enemy ships.

By the fifteenth century, Chinese junks were the largest and most seaworthy ships in the world. These colorful ships had four-sided sails called lugsails, superior rigging, and sternpost rudders. Junks were built with compartmentalized interiors, confining leaks to the breached compartment. Western shipbuilding technology didn't catch up until the nineteenth century.

Sailing Ships

Ships with sails dominated the seas for most of the millennium. Slow but steady improvements in sail design led the way to bigger and faster ships that could cross the oceans.

At the beginning of the millennium, most sailing ships had a square sail held up by a mast. By 1200, the two-masted ship appeared, using a square sail and a lateen sail. By the fifteenth century, ships often had three masts and five or six sails to propel the larger hulls and navigate through all kinds of wind directions.

By the mid-1800s, the largest sailing ships had more than twenty sails and their hulls were built in part of bronze and iron. But with the introduction of the steamboat, the sailing era ended.

Early in the millennium, Europeans used a kind of ship called a cog that had a single large sail and a steering oar on one side.

By the late eighteenth and early nineteenth centuries, huge men-of-war carried massive amounts of guns and sails. They had more than 100 guns arranged on several decks. Fleets of these huge ships were used by countries such as England, France, and Spain to fight wars and to protect trade routes between distant colonies.

Clipper ships were cargo vessels built for speed in the mid-1800s. They sailed trade routes between Europe, North America, and Asia.

Steamboats

The first experimental steamboats appeared in the seventeenth and eighteenth centuries. But mechanical problems hindered their development. Paddles and propellers were not strong enough to push boats containing heavy steam engines. It wasn't until 1803 that Robert Fulton launched the first successful steamboat on the Siene River in France. Fulton had figured out that the paddle wheel was the best way to propel steamboats. In 1807, his ship, the *Clermont*, steamed up the Hudson River from New York City to Albany.

Steamers were often built not only with paddles or propellers, but also with full sails in case of mechanical problems. But by the mid-1800s, ships exclusively using steam power gave sailing ships real competition and ushered in a new shipping era.

Steam turbine engines appeared in 1884, replacing the older reciprocating steam engines. Steam turbines were widely used until the early 1900s. During the 1920s and 1930s, diesel engines, which were more economical to run, began to replace steam turbines.

Side-wheeler steamships (above) had paddle wheels on the sides, while other steamers had paddle wheels on the stern.

Robert Fulton's Clermont *(right) was the first successful commercial steamboat. The 133-foot (41 m) boat had three large cabins, 54 berths, and could travel 3 mph (5 km/h).*

River steamboats (left) used giant paddle wheels for extra power when moving against strong river currents. They also had flat bottoms to prevent becoming stuck in the shallow areas of a river.

Ocean-going steamships of the mid-nineteenth century used propellers instead of side paddles. Propellers worked better in rough water and made better use of the steam power.

16

Oceanliners

By the turn of the twentieth century, passenger liners had grown to huge proportions. The crew of an average oceanliner might number in the hundreds, including cooks, entertainers, and maintenance staff.

During the years after World War II, passenger liners became less important as people began using air transportation to travel across the oceans. At the end of the millennium, many oceanliners were still in use as vacation cruise ships.

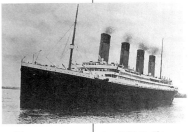

In 1912, the Titanic (above) weighed in at over 46,000 gross tons (46,736 t).

Container ships (left) carry large standard-sized containers in which a variety of cargo can be packed. Containers make loading and unloading cargo faster and easier.

In 1996, the Carnival Destiny (left), was the largest cruise ship ever constructed. It was 892 feet long (272 m) with a maximum passenger capacity of 3,360 and a crew of 1,040.

The hovercraft (right), first operated in 1959, uses fans to lift it above the water. By riding on a cushion of air, a hovercraft can travel much faster than a conventional ship.

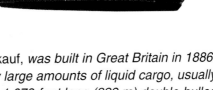

The first tanker, the Glückauf, was built in Great Britain in 1886. Tankers are built to carry large amounts of liquid cargo, usually oil. Mobil Corporation's 1,078-foot long (329 m) double-hulled Raven supertanker (right) carries 2.2 million barrels of oil, enough to fuel 5.7 million vehicles.

TRAINS & MASS TRANSIT

The first trains appeared in European mines around 1550. Horses pulled mining cars with flanged wheels along iron tracks. Less expensive to operate, steam locomotives slowly replaced horses on the mining railways. Steady improvements were made in engine and track design, making the first public railroad possible.

By the 1850s, railroads had spread across Europe and North America. Freight and passengers traveled at unheard-of speeds.

At first, train crashes were common because of poor rail designs. But in the second half of the 1800s, with the development of steel rails, electric block signaling, and air brakes, trains became a fast, reliable, low-cost way of transporting goods and people across countries and continents. The development of subways, streetcars, and cable cars brought railroad transportation to urban areas.

George Stephenson invented a train called the Rocket *(right), in 1829. It had steam-driven pistons that drove the wheels, a boiler, and a smokestack. The general design was followed to the end of the steam era. Stephenson also built the* Stephenson *(left) in 1830.*

Early passenger trains (above) were often stagecoaches and freight wagons equipped with flanged wheels that rode on iron rails.

By the early 1900s, the age of railroads had hit its peak. Thanks to mass production, the automobile became affordable and began replacing trains and streetcars as the most popular mode of transportation. By the mid-1900s, the airplane became the chief means of traveling long distances.

High-speed trains were introduced in Europe and Asia to compete with commercial airplanes. A promising new use of rail technology was the light-rail system, which many large cities adopted.

Steam Trains

In 1804, Richard Trevithick invented the first working steam locomotive, called the *New Castle*, in Wales. The *New Castle* hauled mining cars. English engineer George Stephenson built the first public railway in 1825. It ran between the English towns of Stockton and Darlington.

Steam trains were introduced in the U.S. in the 1800s. On December 25, 1830, the South Carolina Railroad provided the first scheduled steam railway service. Soon, passenger cars evolved from converted stagecoaches to compartments that were enclosed and heated. Locomotives had progressed from wheeled carts with engines to enclosed cars with headlights, whistles, and cowcatchers. The steam era lasted until the emergence of the diesel engine in the early 1900s.

Peter Cooper built America's first locomotive, the Tom Thumb *(right), in 1829. On August 28, 1830, the* Tom Thumb *hauled eighteen directors of the Baltimore and Ohio Railroad in an open car from Baltimore to Ellicott's Mills and back. The B&O became the first U.S. railroad to carry passengers and freight.*

The locomotive Governor Ellis *(right), with its cowcatcher, was built in 1859.*

By transporting people and goods, railroads helped many new towns on the American frontier grow and prosper.

Electric and Diesel Trains

Electric trains were introduced in the latter part of the nineteenth century. They get their power from electrical power lines running overhead. Electric trains are expensive to construct and are usually only built in densely populated areas.

Diesel trains were introduced in the first decade of the twentieth century. They run on diesel engines that drive generators. The generators drive electric motors geared to the locomotive's axles. Because these trains combine the power of diesel and electricity, they are sometimes called diesel-electric locomotives.

Electric and diesel trains were cleaner, quieter, and more efficient than steam-powered trains. By the 1950s, electric and diesel trains had replaced most steam-driven trains.

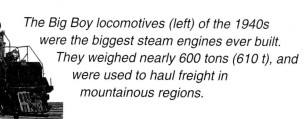

The Big Boy locomotives (left) of the 1940s were the biggest steam engines ever built. They weighed nearly 600 tons (610 t), and were used to haul freight in mountainous regions.

Electric locomotives (below) have a device on top called a pantograph that picks up electric current from overhead wires.

The new General Motors Electro-Motive locomotives (left) are fuel-efficient and better for the environment than older diesel locomotives.

Subways

The first subway was London's Metropolitan Subway (right), which began operating in 1863. The line carried 9,500,000 passengers in its first year of operation. Soon, other major European cities, including Glasgow, Budapest, and Paris, built subways of their own. By 1890, electric engines began replacing steam engines on the underground railway. This eliminated soot and steam pollution in the tunnels.

In 1898, America's first subway opened in Boston. New York City built what would become the world's largest subway system, which opened in 1904.

Throughout the 1900s, increasing automobile traffic forced large cities to either expand existing subway systems or build new ones. By the mid-1950s, Tokyo, Moscow, and Toronto had all built subway systems to aid commuters.

During the second half of the century, subway construction continued as train and track design improved. Cars were lighter and had better suspension, while tracks became smoother, which increased train speed.

San Francisco built the world's first automated subway system in 1972. The trains are computer controlled and operated by remote control. Each train requires only one crewperson in case the computer fails.

The Metro (left), an automated subway system in Washington, D.C., opened in 1976.

City officials get a tour of New York City's first subway in January 1904 (right).

Streetcars and Light-Rail

Streetcars, also called trams and trolly cars, first appeared in the early 1800s. The first streetcars were pulled by horses. Early efforts to replace horse power with electricity were unsuccessful. Batteries were large and expensive. Conducting electricity through the tracks created a shock hazard. Leo Daft and Charles Van Depoele devised methods to transmit power through overhead lines. By the mid-1880s, this system was in use in many U.S. cities. Streetcar systems flourished through the 1920s in major cities worldwide. But then many systems were dismantled to make room for automobile traffic.

Light-rail vehicles (LRVs) evolved from streetcar technology. In North America in the 1980s, LRVs were used to reduce automobile traffic. LRVs are electric rail systems used in large metropolitan areas. They usually use single cars or short trains, which get power from electric lines running overhead or on a third rail running alongside the track. Speeds average 10 to 25 mph (16 to 40 km/h).

A street car in Sarajevo, Bosnia (below)

Many large cities in North America have light-rail transit systems (right), which travel high above the street level in downtown areas.

Cable Cars

Andrew Hallidie invented the cable car in 1867. It ran on a continuously-moving, underground cable, which was propelled by a steam engine. Its pulling power was ideally suited for maneuvering cars on hilly terrain. The first cable car system appeared in 1873 in San Francisco. It was still in use at the end of the millennium.

Another type of cable car is known as an aerial tramway. Tramway cars are supported by continuously-moving, overhead cables suspended by a tower system. Tramways were still used at the end of the millennium to ascend mountains and cross canyons and river gorges.

A San Francisco cable car

Tourists ride a cable car (right) after visiting the Sugarloaf Mountain in Rio de Janeiro, Brazil.

High-Speed Trains

The promise of high-speed commuter trains is to reduce traffic and pollution in densely populated urban areas. Bullet trains were introduced in Japan in 1965. The Tokaido Line between Tokyo and Osaka runs at speeds averaging 103 mph (166 km/h). One of the fastest passenger trains in service at the end of the millennium was Germany's Intercity Express (ICE). By the year 2000, it planned to have trains in service that would reach 186 mph (300 km/h).

Traveling up to 160 mph (260 km/h), a high-speed French Train à Grande Vitesse (TGV) electric train travels through the countryside (above).

A newly-designed bullet train sits to the left of a current type at the Tokyo Station in 1996 (right). The newest bullet trains can speed up to 188 mph (302 km/h) during regular operations.

Automated Guideway Transit

Automated Guideway Transit (AGT) is driverless mass transit that follows fixed guideways. One of the first successful large-scale AGT systems was the Wuppertal *Schwebahn* in Wuppertal, Germany, which began passenger service in 1901. Personal Rapid Transit (PRT) is an AGT system that transports individual parties from one origin to one destination. Group Rapid Transit (GRT) moves large groups of people to a common destination. Monorails and moving walkways are also classified as AGT.

This AGT in New England makes its way down the 800-foot (244 m) track between the Wellington Station stop and a Medford, Massachusetts, parking garage in less than a minute.

BICYCLES & MOTORCYCLES

Early bicycles were novelty items used for amusement. Later, people rode bikes for recreation, sightseeing, exercising, and racing. Design improvements in the 1880s made the bike a practical mode of transportation.

Adding motor power to the bicycle resulted in the invention of the motorcycle. Scooters and mopeds made motorcycle technology available on a much smaller scale.

Bicycles

In 1817, Germany's Baron Karl Friedrich Drais von Sauerbronn built a running machine that was the forerunner of the bicycle. In 1839, Kirkpatrick Macmillan built the first self-propelled bicycle.

In 1861, Frenchmen Pierre and Ernest Michaux developed the penny farthing or high bicycle.

In 1879, Harry J. Lawson designed a chain-driven bicycle that was called the safety bicycle. England's James K. Starley developed the first modern bicycle using this design.

In 1888, John Dunlop patented the pneumatic tire. This made bicycles more comfortable and increased their efficiency. In the 1890s, gears were developed that made bikes easier to ride, particularly uphill.

At the end of the millennium, bicycles were made of lighter, stronger materials and had a variety of accessories. But the bicycle's basic design had changed little since the late 1800s.

Riders sat on the running machine (below) and pushed it along with their feet.

Macmillan's bicycle (above) had two swinging cranks that moved rods attached to the rear wheel.

The pedals were attached to the big front wheel on the high bicycle (right). The big wheel allowed the bike to go a long way with each turn of the pedals.

The safety bicycle (above) had a chain driving the rear wheel. The pedals and sprocket were located under the seat. The tires were the same size and made of solid rubber.

Modern bicycles (left) use the same design as the nineteenth century safety bicycle.

Motorcycles

In the 1860s, inventors applied motor power to the bicycle. This allowed bicycle riders to travel farther with less effort.

The first motorcycle with an internal combustion engine was built in Germany in 1885 by Gottlieb Daimler.

Before World War I, motorcycle manufacturers made significant advancements in design and performance. During the war, motorcycles were used by European armed forces. After the war, motorcycles were popular for transportation and racing until the Great Depression.

During World War II, the Allies realized the value of motorcycle transportation in combat and manufacturers made thousands of military motorcycles.

When the war ended, vehicles and gas were in short supply. People needed cheap, fuel-efficient transportation. In Japan, Honda began producing clean, high-quality, reliable bikes. In 1947, Vespa and Lambretta began producing scooters in Italy. Germany produced the moped.

As economies improved and more people could afford cars, world motorcycle production declined. But as the millennium ended, motorcycles were still popular for transportation that was reliable, cheap, and fun.

Daimler's motorcycle had advanced features such as twist-grip controls and linked steering.

Big-bike manufacturers Harley-Davidson and Indian made full-sized military bikes like the Indian 841 (above).

Scooters and mopeds, like this Italian Vespa (left) and Austrian Puch (right), are useful for short trips in small, crowded urban areas.

American motorcycle makers such as Harley-Davidson, Indian, and Excelsior-Henderson excelled at making "big bikes," large motorcycles (below) equipped for long-distance touring.

Japan's motorcycle companies dominate the world market. The Honda C100 Cub (right) was introduced in 1956. It is the bestselling motorcycle ever made.

AUTOMOBILES

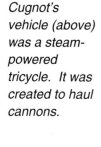

In 1769, Frenchman Nicolas-Joseph Cugnot operated the first self-propelled vehicle. It was difficult to control and soon crashed, but experiments with automobiles continued.

By 1885 two German inventors, Karl Benz and Gottlieb Daimler, had both produced gas-engined cars. The automobile's hauling power was soon realized when gas-powered trucks and buses were created in the 1890s.

In the following years, automobile engineers continued to experiment, making automobiles easier to operate and more comfortable. By the end of the millennium, automobiles had evolved into technically advanced vehicles.

Cugnot's vehicle (above) was a steam-powered tricycle. It was created to haul cannons.

In 1885, Benz built a three-wheeled vehicle (left), while Daimler's 1885 vehicle looked like a horseless carriage (right).

1900s

At the turn of the century, automobiles were powered by gas, electric, or steam engines. Automobiles were not fully enclosed. They had kerosene-powered headlights and bulb horns. The parts used in automobiles were handmade to fit each individual car. This changed in 1908 when American Henry M. Leland came up with the idea to standardize parts, which aided in the mass production of automobiles.

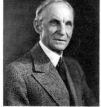

Henry Ford built the first Model T in 1908.

The Stanley steamer (above), a light steam-powered American car, held the world speed record in 1906 at 127 mph (204 km/h).

1910s

During the 1910s, cars became more practical. Electric ignitions were introduced and cars became fully enclosed, which protected drivers and passengers from the elements. In 1914, Henry Ford created an assembly line to mass produce his car, the Model T. Assembly-line construction reduced the cost of cars, allowing average workers to afford them.

In 1912, Cadillac produced the first car with an electric starter (above), liberating drivers from the labor-intensive hand crank starters.

1920s

In the 1920s, people placed more emphasis on the car's style, favoring large and luxurious vehicles. One such luxury was the car radio, which was first offered as an option by Philadelphia Storage Battery Corporation in 1927. Other innovations of the decade included the introduction of safety glass and Duesenburg's introduction of four-wheel hydraulic brakes.

Ford's Model T (above) made up nearly half of the world's cars in the early 1920s.

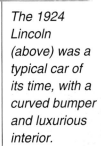

The 1924 Lincoln (above) was a typical car of its time, with a curved bumper and luxurious interior.

1930s

During the 1930s, automobile makers refined cars, making them more technically advanced. Independent front suspension and front wheel drive became common features. And by the 1930s, the internal combustion gasoline engine had replaced steam and electric engines in new automobiles.

In 1932, Henry Ford became the first person to mass-produce V-8 engines, making them affordable to average workers. These powerful engines were first offered in Ford's 1932 models (right).

Oldsmobile introduced the world's first fully automatic transmission in its 1940 models (above).

1940s

New car production came to a near standstill during the 1940s because of World War II. But after the war, car production resumed and an increasing number of Americans bought automobiles. New car buyers of the 1940s could select from several options to make their cars more comfortable, such as heaters, air conditioners, windshield wipers, and automatic transmissions.

In 1948, Preston Tucker created the Tucker Torpedo (left). The car had many advanced features, such as fuel injection, independent suspension, disc brakes, and a popout windshield.

1950s

As car ownership increased after World War II, people started to make their homes further away from their workplaces. Suburbs grew in the United States and Canada as people used their cars to escape city life. Power brakes and power steering became standard on most cars, and Mercedes-Benz had introduced fuel-injection.

In Europe during the 1950s, fuel was expensive. Cars like the Fiat 500 (left) became popular because they were small and fuel-efficient.

During the 1950s, cars in North America, like the Buick Le Sabre (above), grew large and roomy with tail fins.

In the 1960s, fuel remained cheap in the United States. Sporty, gas-guzzling cars like the 1965 Ford Mustang (below) were popular.

1960s

Automobile makers did not actively address the issue of safety until the 1960s. Seat belts were one of the first required safety devices. By 1964, lap belts were standard in front seats. In 1968, the American government required all new cars to have shoulder harnesses attached to the lap belts in the front seat.

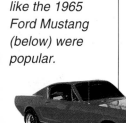

In the 1960s, the U.S. interstate highway system (left) grew into a 42,500-mile (68,380 km) network of roads, making travel faster and easier.

28

1970s

The oil embargo of the 1970s raised gasoline prices in America, making the gas-guzzling cars of the past very expensive to fuel. As a result, people wanted small, aerodynamic, fuel-efficient cars. People also started to become concerned about car emissions, which cause air pollution. By the mid-1970s, emission controlling devices were required on all automobiles made in the United States.

During the 1970s, the Honda Civic (above) sold well in the U.S. because of its fuel-efficiency.

1980s

By the mid-1980s, most new cars had air conditioning, automatic transmissions, and radios as standard equipment. Safety devices continued to improve with innovations such as the motorized automatic seat belt, introduced by Toyota in 1980. A year later, General Motors and Chrysler offered cars with microprocessors.

To compete with the increasing number of Japanese imports, American automobile makers began producing their own medium-sized, fuel-efficient cars such as the 1981 Dodge Aries (left).

1990s

Automotive safety played a large role in the car designs of the 1990s. Several luxury options became available on automobiles, such as CD players, dual zone climate controls, and global positioning systems.

The emergence of new luxury automobiles from Japan, such as the Lexus (left), fueled the automobile industry's success in the 1990s.

Safety devices such as airbags (below) and antilock brakes became standard features on most new cars at the end of the millennium.

At the end of the millennium, cars such as the Volkswagen Beetle were redesigned to be rounder and more aerodynamic.

Trucks

Shortly after motorized vehicles were invented, people realized their potential for hauling heavy loads of freight. In 1896, Gottlieb Daimler built the first motorized truck (left). Trucks were first widely used during World War I.

During the 1920s, the trucking industry grew as roads improved and trucks were equipped with pneumatic tires and air brakes.

In 1910, White Motor Company built steam-powered freight wagons (above).

As they began hauling heavier loads, trucks needed a stronger engine. So, after World War II, trucks started using diesel engines, which were more powerful than gasoline engines. Many of the advances made in car design, such as power steering, independent suspension, and emissions controls, were transferred to trucks.

Heavy-duty trucks weigh more than 33,000 pounds (14,969 kg) and can be single-unit vehicles or cabs with semitrailers. They are the big freight haulers that transport goods from city to city. Heavy-duty trucks also include off-road construction vehicles and mining trucks.

Light-duty trucks are single-unit vehicles that weigh up to 14,000 pounds (6,350 kg). This includes vans, pickups, and sport utility vehicles (SUVs).

Pickup trucks, like the 1988 Dodge Power Wagon (right), grew in popularity throughout the 1980s.

In 1984, Chrysler introduced the first minivans, the Dodge Caravan (above) and the Plymouth Voyager.

The popularity of SUV's (right) helped boost sales of light-duty trucks in North America at the end of the millennium.

Today, most heavy-duty trucks use turbocharged diesel engines. With the growth of the interstate highway system in the 1960s, freight transport by truck in North America became more and more important, at the expense of the railroad industry.

Buses

The first buses were large, steam-powered stagecoaches that appeared in England in the 1830s. In 1895 the first gasoline-powered bus was created. It was built in Germany and could carry eight passengers.

Early buses were constructed by mounting a bus body onto a truck chassis. In 1921, American engineers designed a wider, longer, and lower chassis made specifically for buses. Other improvements followed, including the use of the diesel engine and air suspension.

The main types of buses in service at the end of the millennium were city, suburban, tour, and school. Buses aid in energy conservation while reducing traffic and air pollution.

School buses (left) have special safety features like stop signs that extend, allowing children to cross the street safely.

An omnibus of the early 20th century

Double-decker buses are popular in London, England (above), while large coaches work well for tour groups (right).

Pilâtre de Rozier and d'Arlandes ascend in a hot air balloon in 1783.

AIRCRAFT & SPACECRAFT

In 1783, French aeronauts Jean-François Pilâtre de Rozier and Marquis François Laurent d'Arlandes were the first humans to ascend in a hot air balloon. Soon inventors were dreaming of flight in which they could control an aircraft's direction, rather than rely on the whims of the wind.

Inventors experimented with aircraft such as airships and gliders. And by the early twentieth century, flexible-winged gliders had given way to fixed-wing airplanes with small gasoline-powered engines. The era of pilot-controlled flight had begun.

In just over 100 years, airplanes have allowed people to cross continents and oceans in a fraction of the time it takes using ground transportation. Modern jets and airplanes can achieve speeds three times faster than sound, and can carry tons of material and hundreds of people.

Hot Air Balloons

Except for limited military use toward the end of the nineteenth century, the hot air balloon never caught on as a transportation vehicle. Varying weather conditions and wind speeds made balloons difficult to steer. At the end of the millennium, Bertrand Piccard of Switzerland and Brian Jones of Great Britain successfully circumnavigated the world in their hot air balloon, the *Breitling Orbiter 3*.

The Breitling Orbiter 3 *took off from the Swiss Alps on March 1, 1999.*

At the end of the millennium, hot air balloons served as recreational vehicles for the not so faint-of-heart.

Gliders

By the 1870s, inventors were experimenting with different types of gliders. Gliders use rising columns of air to ascend and planes of air to sustain flight. Gliders greatly helped in the development of airworthy wing designs. At the end of the millennium, gliders were extremely light and could travel for hundreds of miles.

Otto Lilienthal (above) was the first person to achieve pilot-controlled flight with a glider in Germany in 1891.

A modern glider

Airships

The first airship (right), also called a blimp, was invented in 1852 by French engineer Henri Giffard. Airships were a popular way for people to cross the oceans during the 1920s and 1930s. But the airship could not compete with the much faster and safer airplane, which began transatlantic flights in 1939. At the end of the millennium, airships were used for observation and advertisement.

Goodyear blimps (below) act as observation vehicles for televised sporting events. The blimps are filled with nonflammable helium.

The rigid-frame German airship Graf Zeppelin *(right) was huge and luxurious, with a length of 772 feet (235 m). Filled with hydrogen, it flew across the Atlantic Ocean 139 times.*

The age of giant airships ended on May 6, 1937, when the hydrogen-filled Hindenburg *(left) burst into flames, killing 36 people.*

Early Planes

Invented in the early 1900s, the first airplanes were made of birch and canvas and were powered by gas-burning piston engines. Because these planes had two wings, one above the other, they were called biplanes. The first single-winged plane, called a monoplane, appeared in 1907 in France.

By 1914, the first commercial airplane service was operating in Florida. The first commercial airline was established in 1919 in Germany. More soon followed. The flight routes were short, often from city to city within the same region. A typical airplane could only handle a few passengers.

The next big leap in aviation came in 1927 when Charles Lindbergh flew nonstop from New York City to Paris. That year, the U.S. government began transporting mail between distant cities via airplanes. The following year, a commercial link between Chicago and San Francisco was established. The trip took 23 hours.

On December 17, 1903, Orville and Wilbur Wright (left) achieved the first pilot-controlled, powered flight at Kitty Hawk, North Carolina (right). The plane was called the Flyer I. *The flight lasted 12 seconds, covering a distance of about 120 feet (37 m).*

In 1916, Boeing made its first plane (below). It was made of wood, linen, and wire.

The Blackburn Monoplane of 1912 (above) was one of the first single-winged planes to take flight.

In the next few years, coast-to-coast travel and mail service were established in America. Plane design continued to improve, and aircraft grew sturdier, larger, faster, and more aerodynamic.

The world's first modern passenger transport appeared in the early 1930s when the Boeing aircraft company introduced its 247. It had retractable landing gear, smooth all-metal construction, single cantilevered wings—and it could fly 70 mph (113 km/h) faster than its competition. Regularly scheduled passenger service from Chicago to New York was now possible. Late in the decade, the Douglas DC-3 dominated commercial aviation with its greater size and speed.

As the 1940s began, the Boeing 314 flying boat, better known as a "clipper," started regularly scheduled flights across the Pacific Ocean. And its Stratoliner became the first commercial airplane that could fly in high altitudes because of its pressurized cabin. World War II temporarily halted further development of commercial aircraft.

Charles A. Lindbergh (left) flew the Spirit of St. Louis *(right) nonstop from New York City to Paris May 20 to 21, 1927. It was the first successful nonstop flight across the Atlantic Ocean, and it paved the way for transatlantic commercial flights.*

The Douglas DC-3 (right) carried 21 passengers and could cross the United States in less than 24 hours (with fuel stops). By 1939, the DC-3 handled 90 percent of the world's passenger traffic, and became the bestselling commercial aircraft in history.

The 1946 four-engine DC-4 (right) carried 44 passengers at more than 200 mph (321 km/h) and was three times the size of the DC-3.

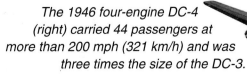

Jet Planes

The era of commercial jets began in 1949 with the de Havilland Comet, which experienced some success in Europe. The Boeing 707 appeared in America in 1957, followed by the larger Douglas DC-8 a year later. Both jets had four engines, and could fly more than 600 mph (965 km/h).

The 727, with its T-tail and aft-mounted engines, entered service in 1964. Douglas countered with the DC-9, which became the second-best-selling jetliner in history.

The most successful commercial jet plane, the 737, was introduced in 1967. It could carry more passengers than the DC-9.

The biggest advancement in jetliners came in 1969 when the 747 appeared. It was 225 feet long (69 m) and stood as tall as a six-story building. Because the 747 could carry 374 passengers, it greatly reduced the per-ticket cost, which made flying more affordable for a greater number of people. Boeing's newest commercial jetliner, the 777, appeared in 1995.

Besides their use as commercial aircraft, jets were also used as private planes and as a means to transport cargo.

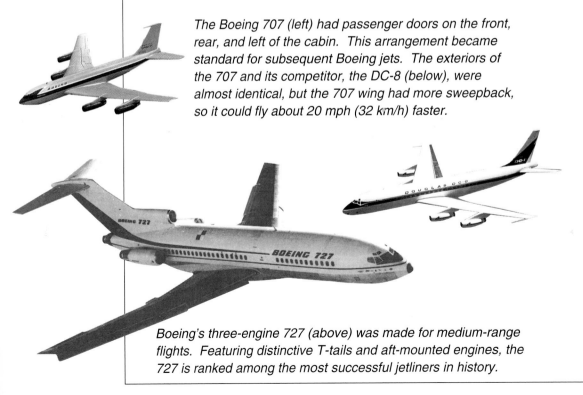

The Boeing 707 (left) had passenger doors on the front, rear, and left of the cabin. This arrangement became standard for subsequent Boeing jets. The exteriors of the 707 and its competitor, the DC-8 (below), were almost identical, but the 707 wing had more sweepback, so it could fly about 20 mph (32 km/h) faster.

Boeing's three-engine 727 (above) was made for medium-range flights. Featuring distinctive T-tails and aft-mounted engines, the 727 is ranked among the most successful jetliners in history.

Boeing's 737 (right) was designed to shuttle passengers between nearby cities. Since then, nearly 200 customers in every corner of the world have ordered the 737. With more than 2,800 airplanes delivered, the 737 is the bestselling jetliner in history.

The Boeing 747-400 (above) can carry more than 400 people without stopping for more than 8,470 miles (13,600 km). Turbofan jet engines propel these jumbo jets to more than 500 mph (805 km/h).

The twin-engine, medium-range 757 (left) is more fuel efficient than the older 727 jetliners it was designed to replace, but it retains the 727's short-field capability. The 757 carries up to 239 passengers and has a range of approximately 4,500 miles (7,240 km).

As the world's largest twinjet, the Boeing 777 (right) carries 305 to 440 people and has a range of 4,560 miles (7,337 km).

The British-French Concorde supersonic transport (right) began carrying passengers in 1976. It can travel at twice the speed of sound.

The Learjet (right) is one of the most successful private jets in history.

Breaking the Sound Barrier

On October 14, 1947, test pilot Chuck Yeager (left) became the fastest person on Earth when he broke the sound barrier in his experimental rocket-powered Bell X-1 aircraft (below). Many people thought planes could never fly faster than sound (769 mph [1,237 km/h]).

Jet Engines

There are three common types of jet engines: the turbojet, turboprop, and turbofan. All work on the principle of mixing compressed air with fuel, creating large amounts of thrust that propel jet aircraft at high speeds.

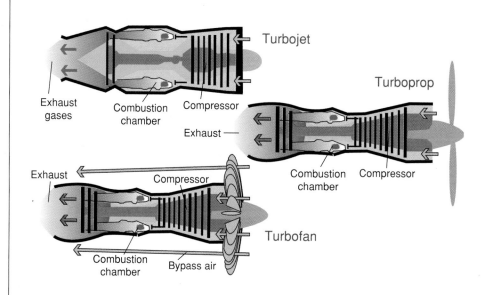

Turbojet

Exhaust gases   Combustion chamber   Compressor

Turboprop

Exhaust   Combustion chamber   Compressor

Exhaust   Compressor   Turbofan

Combustion chamber   Bypass air

Helicopters

Frenchman Paul Cornu made the first vertical flight in a helicopter in 1907. But his flight lasted only 20 seconds and reached a height of one foot. Engines were not powerful enough to keep the machines airborne. That changed in 1939, when American Igor Sikorsky successfully tested his VS-300. His design, a three-blade main rotor and tail rotor, set the standards for rapid development worldwide.

After World War II, helicopters were used for a number of commercial applications, such as search and rescue, fire fighting, crop spraying, and medical evacuation. The Bell Aircraft Corporation led the way with their successful two-blade rotor helicopter, the Bell Model 47. Tandem-rotor helicopters also appeared, which allowed greater overall size and lift capacity. Jet engine technology was added in 1951 to give the helicopter greater speed and even more lift capacity. Basic helicopter design remained the same at the end of the millennium.

Amelia Earhart set the women's autogiro altitude record at 18,451 feet (5,624 m) in 1931.

The autogiro (right) was invented by Spain's Juan de la Cierva and made its first successful flight in 1923. It was the forerunner of the helicopter, with a propeller that provided forward movement and rotating blades that provided lift.

Igor Sikorsky flew the first modern helicopter, the VS-300 (left), in 1939.

The Bell Model 47 (above) was the first two-blade rotor helicopter.

The Sikorsky S-92 (right) serves international utility and commercial needs, including passenger, cargo, and rescue.

The *Freedom 7*
space capsule
(above) and its
launch vehicle, a
Redstone rocket
(below)

Spacecraft

The first manned spacecraft, the space capsule *Vostok I*, was launched on April 12, 1961 by the Soviet Union. Cosmonaut Yuri A. Gagarin was the first human to enter space.

Alan B. Shepard, Jr., was the first American to enter space. He flew a suborbital flight on May 5, 1961, in the Mercury space capsule *Freedom 7*, which was launched atop a Redstone rocket. Space capsules were the predominant vehicle for space travel until the United States launched the first space shuttle, *Columbia*, on April 12, 1981.

The shuttle was originally designed mainly to put satellites into orbit. Today, it has a wide range of missions, including putting scientists into orbit to study space and transporting sections of the International Space Station.

Space shuttles are made up of three main parts: a reusable orbiter, two solid-propellant rocket boosters, and a large liquid-propellant tank. The orbiter is designed to last for around one hundred flights. It carries payload in a large mid-fuselage bay that measures 15 x 60 feet (4.6 x 18 m).

After completing its mission, a space shuttle re-enters Earth's atmosphere, then acts like a glider, making an unpowered landing on a runway.

*Alan B. Shepard
(right) was the
first American in
space.*

*Soviet Air Force Major Yuri A. Gagarin
(above) became the first space traveler
in history on April 12, 1961. Gagarin
made the historic flight in the space
capsule* Vostok 1 *(right), which traveled
at 18,000 mph (28,962 km/h) and
stayed in orbit for an hour and three
quarters before making a safe landing in
a predetermined area.*

Astronauts Neil Armstrong, left, Michael Collins, center, and Edwin Aldrin, right, are pictured in this 1969 Apollo 11 crew portrait (above). Armstrong was the first human to step on the moon's surface. Apollo 11 was propelled into space by a Saturn IV rocket (right).

Astronaut James Irwin salutes a U.S. flag planted on the surface of the moon during the Apollo 15 mission in August, 1971 (right). The Apollo missions' lunar module, center, and the lunar rover, right, were the first vehicles to transport people to and on the moon.

A space shuttle blasts off like a rocket (right) but lands like an airplane (below). Fully loaded with fuel, it weighs up to 4.5 million pounds (2 million kg).

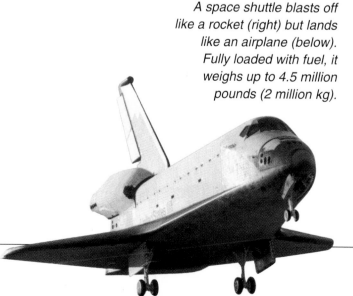

TRANSPORTATION

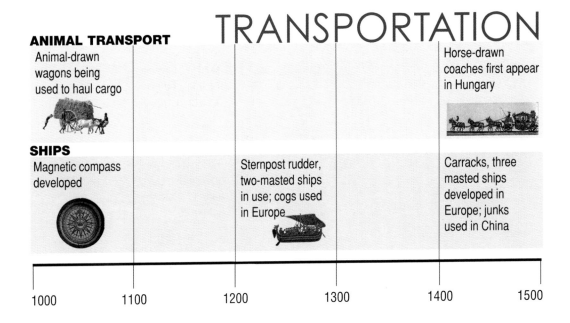

ANIMAL TRANSPORT

Animal-drawn wagons being used to haul cargo

Horse-drawn coaches first appear in Hungary

SHIPS

Magnetic compass developed

Sternpost rudder, two-masted ships in use; cogs used in Europe

Carracks, three masted ships developed in Europe; junks used in China

| 1000 | 1100 | 1200 | 1300 | 1400 | 1500 |

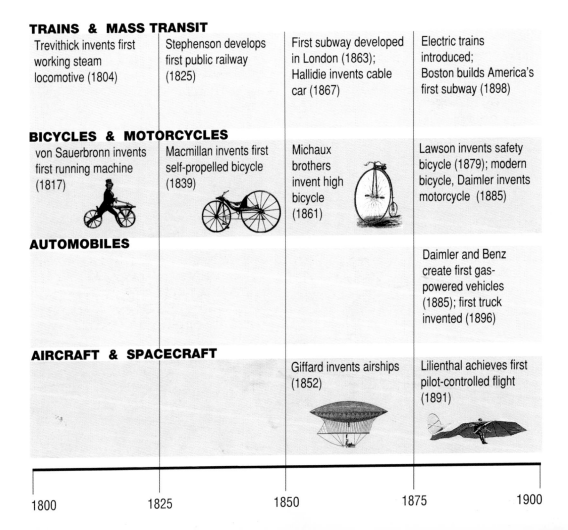

TRAINS & MASS TRANSIT

Trevithick invents first working steam locomotive (1804)

Stephenson develops first public railway (1825)

First subway developed in London (1863); Hallidie invents cable car (1867)

Electric trains introduced; Boston builds America's first subway (1898)

BICYCLES & MOTORCYCLES

von Sauerbronn invents first running machine (1817)

Macmillan invents first self-propelled bicycle (1839)

Michaux brothers invent high bicycle (1861)

Lawson invents safety bicycle (1879); modern bicycle, Daimler invents motorcycle (1885)

AUTOMOBILES

Daimler and Benz create first gas-powered vehicles (1885); first truck invented (1896)

AIRCRAFT & SPACECRAFT

Giffard invents airships (1852)

Lilienthal achieves first pilot-controlled flight (1891)

| 1800 | 1825 | 1850 | 1875 | 1900 |

MILESTONES

ANIMAL TRANSPORT

Horses brought to the Americas by Spanish conquistadores 	Glass windows added to coaches; Berlin coach invented (1660)	Coaches, Conestoga wagons appear in America	Stagecoach service begins in America; buggies appear in America	

SHIPS

			Fulton launches first steamboat; steam turbine engines introduced	Age of oceanliners begins; container ships developed

1500   1600   1700   1800   1900   2000

TRAINS & MASS TRANSIT

New York City subway opens (1904)	Big Boy locomotives appear	Tokyo, Moscow, and Toronto have all opened subway systems; first bullet train in Japan (1965)	First automated subway built in San Francisco (1972)

BICYCLES & MOTORCYCLES

BMW makes first moped	Vespa and Lambretta begin making scooters in Italy (1947)	Honda introduces the C-100 Cub (1956)	

AUTOMOBILES

Cadillac first to use electric starters (1912); Ford creates automobile assembly line (1914)	First car radios (1927); automatic transmission introduced (1940)	Small cars become popular in Europe; shoulder-harness seat belts required in American-made cars (1968)	Gas crisis makes small cars popular in the U.S.; emission control devices appear; SUVs become popular

AIRCRAFT & SPACECRAFT

First powered flight in biplane (1903); first helicopter flight (1907)	First transatlantic flight (1927); first passenger airplane appears (1933); modern helicopter invented (1939); first commercial jet (1949)	First space capsule launched (1961); humans land on the moon (1969)	First supersonic transport (1976); first space shuttle launched (1981)

1900   1925   1950   1975   2000

GLOSSARY

A.D. - a designation of time, used in expressing dates after the birth of Christ. The abbreviation A.D. stands for the Latin words *Anno Domini,* meaning "in the year of the Lord."

aerodynamic - a design that reduces air resistance. It allows automobiles, trains, and aircraft to travel faster and use fuel more efficiently.

aeronaut - a person who operates or travels in an airship or hot air balloon.

aft-mounted - anything placed toward the tail of an aircraft or the stern of a ship.

air brakes - a braking system that uses air pressure to stop a moving vehicle. This system is used on trains, trucks, and buses.

air suspension - a suspension system with pressurized, air-filled springs. The springs easily adjust to changes in weight, keeping the vehicle level and at the same height. This system is mainly used on buses.

airship - any aircraft that gets its lift from lighter-than-air gases.

axle - a bar on which a wheel turns.

B.C. - a designation of time, used in expressing dates before the birth of Christ. The abbreviation B.C. stands for "before Christ."

blimp - a type of airship. Its frame is made of cables covered with fabric, and it's filled with lighter-than-air gases.

breached - an area that has been broken, torn, split, or cracked.

cantilevered wing - the wing of an airplane that is firmly supported at one end and free at the other end.

caravan - a group of people traveling together over a long distance, often through difficult or dangerous regions.

chassis - the framework of a vehicle that connects the body, wheels, and engine.

circumnavigate - to travel completely around the earth.

compartmentalize - to divide into separate compartments or sections.

cowcatcher - a metal frame on the front of a train that clears obstacles from the tracks.

diesel engine - an internal combustion engine that uses hot, pressurized air to ignite the fuel.

disc brakes - a braking system that uses heat-resistant pads and a disc attached to the wheel.

dual zone climate control - a system that allows a passenger to control the temperature of his or her space within an automobile.

electric block signaling - a type of railroad communication in which the track is divided into several blocks. An electrical unit oversees each block and allows only one train to pass through at a time, reducing accidents.

embargo - limits placed on the import, export, or sale of goods.

emission - the gasses released when an engine runs.

flanged - when a rim attaches one object to another. Train wheels are flanged so they stay on the tracks.

front wheel drive - when the front axles turn and drive the front wheels.

fuel injection - an electronic system that supplies a fuel and air mixture directly into the engine in controlled amounts. It improves fuel efficiency and vehicle performance.

fuselage - the central area of an airplane or shuttle used for the crew or cargo.

gasoline engine - an internal combustion engine that uses spark plugs to ignite the fuel.

global positioning system - a satellite-based system that tracks a driver's location on an electronic map in the automobile. This makes it easier for the driver to navigate in unfamiliar places.

hydraulic brakes - a braking system where pressurized fluid stops the automobile. The system is powered by the pressure of the driver's foot on the brake pedal.

ignition - the device used to start an engine. It is also called a starter.

internal combustion - an engine that burns fuel internally and gets power when exploding fuel-air mixture forces pistons down against the crankshaft, which changes this up-and-down motion to a circular motion that turns the wheels.

linked steering - a steering system in which the handlebars or steering wheel is connected to the axle or front wheel by a series of connecting rods and bolts.

microprocessor - a computer processor contained on an integrated circuit chip. When a microprocessor controls a vehicle's ignition and fuel system, emissions are reduced and fuel efficiency increases.

nomad - a person who has no fixed residence and moves about seasonally, usually in search of food.

payload - the load carried by a vehicle that is not necessary for the vehicle's operation.

piston - the part of an engine that compresses the fuel-air mixture within the cylinder.

pneumatic tire - a tire that is filled with compressed air.

power brakes - a system that aids in the stopping of an automobile by using a low-pressure vacuum that is powered by the engine to increase the pressure applied to the brakes when the driver depresses the brake pedal.

power steering - a system that aids in the steering of an automobile by using a hydraulic device that is powered by the engine to increase the pressure that is applied to the steering wheel by the driver.

reciprocating steam engine - a steam engine with pistons and cylinders. Pressurized steam is put into the cylinder by a valve. The steam expands and pushes the piston, which is connected to a crank that produces rotary motion.

retractable landing gear - landing gear is the part of the airplane that supports its weight when it is on the ground. Retractable landing gear moves out of the plane's fuselage when it lands and goes back in after the plane takes off.

rudder - a structure on a ship or plane that, when turned, causes the front of the vehicle to move in that same direction. Sternpost rudders are attached to the sternpost, the principal member of the stern of a ship that extends from the keel to the deck.

running gear - the working and carrying parts of a machine.

saddlery - articles used on a saddle horse, such as harness, saddle, bridle, and bit.

safety glass - glass that is made of a piece of transparent plastic laminated between two pieces of regular glass. Safety glass will not shatter when broken.

sound barrier - a sudden, large increase in aerodynamic drag that occurs as the speed of an aircraft approaches the speed of sound.

steam turbine engine - a rotary engine that gets power from steam passing by vanes on a spindle.

suborbital - less that one full orbit. If a spacecraft flying around the earth does not go all the way around at least once, it has made a suborbital flight.

supersonic transport - transportation that moves from one to five times the speed of sound.

suspension - a system of components such as straps, springs, struts, and shock absorbers that support the body of a vehicle on its frame. If a car has independent suspension, each of the car's wheels has its own suspension components.

sweepback - the backward slant of a cantilevered airplane wing that makes the tip of the wing downstream from the part that is attached to the fuselage. This reduces air resistance and increases speed.

T-tail - a high-level, horizontal stabilizer atop a plane's rudder.

tandem-rotor helicopter - a helicopter with two rotors working together.

technology - the use of scientific knowledge to solve practical problems, especially in industry.

transatlantic - crossing or extending across the Atlantic Ocean.

transmission - a system of gears that transmits power from the engine to the drive axle. Automatic transmissions automatically shift to higher gears as the engine speed increases or decreases. Manual transmissions must be shifted by the driver.

via - by way of. How something gets somewhere.

INTERNET SITES

U.S. Department of Transportation
http://www.dot.gov/
This site presents information on the U.S. Department of Transportation (DOT), which is in charge of building and maintaining a safe and efficient transportation system for the United States.

The Aviation History On-Line Museum
http://www.aviation-history.com/
This informative site includes details of important aircraft and pilots, including the early years of aviation history.

United States Naval & Shipbuilding Museum
http://www.uss-salem.org/
This online museum includes information on naval history and shipbuilding techniques, with over 6,000 ship histories included.

Henry Ford Museum & Greenfield Village
http://www.hfmgv.org/index.html
This site has information on Henry Ford and the development of the automobile. Online exhibits include photos of important American cars.

These sites are subject to change. Go to your favorite search engine and type "transportation" for more sites.

FOR FURTHER READING

Bendick, Jeanne and Sal Murdocca. *Eureka! It's an Automobile!* Brookfield, Connecticut: Millbrook Press, 1994.

Berliner, Don. *Aviation: Reaching for the Sky.* Minneapolis, Minnesota: Oliver Press, 1997.

Humble, Richard. *Submarines and Ships.* New York: Viking Children's Books, 1997.

Wilson, Anthony. *Visual Timelines of Transportation.* London: DK Publishing, 1995.

Wormser, Richard. *The Iron Horse: How Railroads Changed America.* New York: Walker & Company, 1993.

INDEX